PIANO · VOCAL · GUITAR

Disney LOVE SONGS

2ND EDITION

D0927260

The following songs are the property of:

Bourne Co.
Music Publishers
5West 37th Street
New York, NY 10018

I'M WISHING
SOME DAY MY PRINCE WILL COME

ISBN 978-0-793-58021-7

WALT DISNEY MUSIC COMPANY
WONDERLAND MUSIC COMPANY, INC.

DISTRIBUTED BY

HAL•LEONARD®
CORPORATION

7777 W. BLUEMOUND RD. P.O. BOX 13819 MILWAUKEE, WI 53213

In Australia Contact:
Hal Leonard Australia Pty. Ltd.
4 Lentara Court
Cheltenham, Victoria, 3192 Australia
Email: ausadmin@halleonard.com.au

Visit Hal Leonard Online at
www.halleonard.com

BEAUTY AND THE BEAST

from Walt Disney's BEAUTY AND THE BEAST

Lyrics by HOWARD ASHMAN
Music by ALAN MENKEN

CANDLE ON THE WATER

from Walt Disney's PETE'S DRAGON

Words and Music by AL KASHA
and JOEL HIRSCHHORN

I'll be your can-dle on the wa-ter, my love for you will al-ways
I'll be your can-dle on the wa-ter 'til ev-'ry wave is warm and

burn. I know you're lost and drift-ing, but the clouds are lift-ing.
bright. My soul is there be-side you, let this can-dle guide you;

Don't give up; you have some-where to turn.
soon you'll see a gold-en stream of light.

BELLA NOTTE
(This Is the Night)
from Walt Disney's LADY AND THE TRAMP

Words and Music by PEGGY LEE
and SONNY BURKE

Slowly

This _____ is the night, _____ it's a beau - ti - ful night, _____ and we

call it Bel - la Not - te. Look _____ at the skies; _____ they have

stars _____ in their eyes _____ on this love - ly Bel - la Not - te. { So

CAN YOU FEEL THE LOVE TONIGHT

from Walt Disney Pictures' THE LION KING

Music by ELTON JOHN
Lyrics by TIM RICE

I'M WISHING

from Walt Disney's SNOW WHITE AND THE SEVEN DWARFS

Words by LARRY MOREY
Music by FRANK CHURCHILL

IF I NEVER KNEW YOU
(Love Theme from POCAHONTAS)
from Walt Disney's POCAHONTAS

Music by ALAN MENKEN
Lyrics by STEPHEN SCHWARTZ

29

LAVENDER BLUE
(Dilly Dilly)
from Walt Disney's SO DEAR TO MY HEART

Words by LARRY MOREY
Music by ELIOT DANIEL

ONCE UPON A DREAM

from Walt Disney's SLEEPING BEAUTY

Words and Music by SAMMY FAIN
and JACK LAWRENCE
Adapted from a Theme by TCHAIKOVSKY

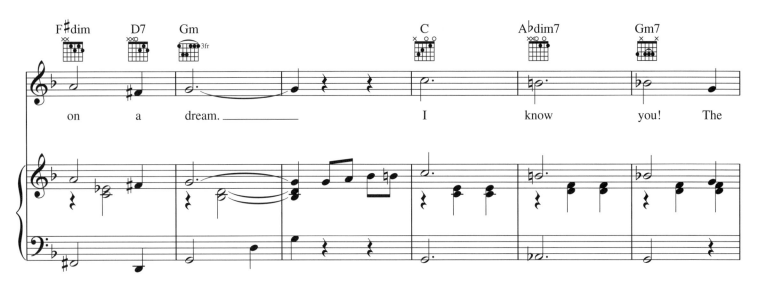

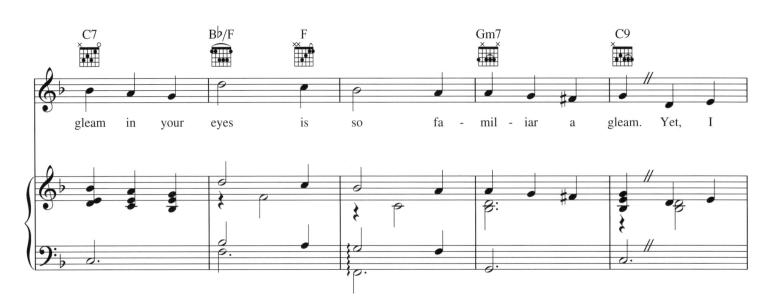

SO DEAR TO MY HEART

from Walt Disney's SO DEAR TO MY HEART

Words by IRVING TAYLOR
Music by TICKER FREEMAN

Some - times I let my fan - cy wan - der _____ 'cross the

vale of by - gone years. And through the mist a - way off

yon - der, _____ a fa - mil - iar world ap - pears. _____ So dear to my

SO THIS IS LOVE
(The Cinderella Waltz)
from Walt Disney's CINDERELLA

Words and Music by MACK DAVID,
AL HOFFMAN and JERRY LIVINGSTON

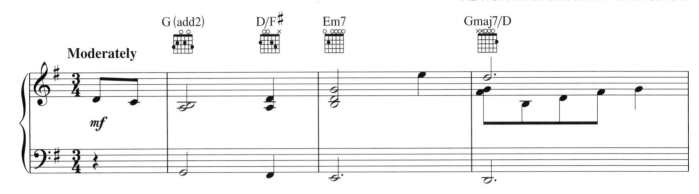

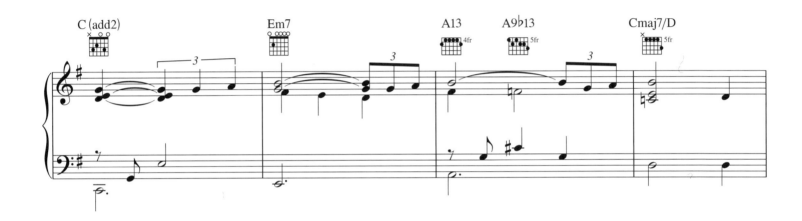

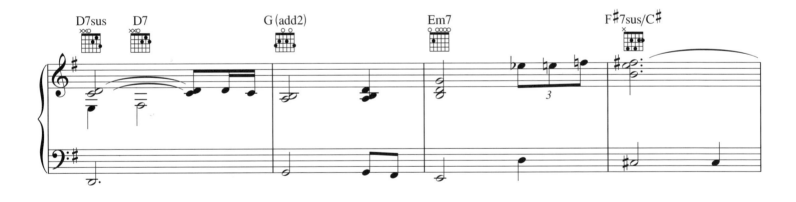

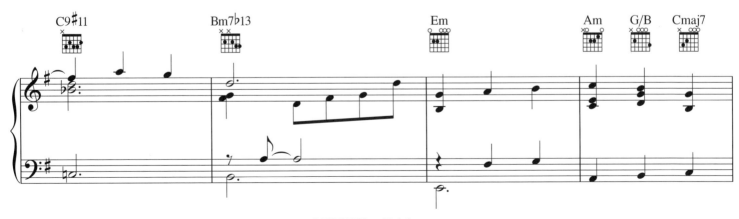

SOME DAY MY PRINCE WILL COME

from Walt Disney's SNOW WHITE AND THE SEVEN DWARFS

Words by LARRY MOREY
Music by FRANK CHURCHILL

THESE ARE THE BEST TIMES

from Walt Disney Productions' SUPERDAD

Words and Music by
SHANE TATUM

A WHOLE NEW WORLD

(Aladdin's Theme)
from Walt Disney's ALADDIN

Music by ALAN MENKEN
Lyrics by TIM RICE

WRITTEN IN THE STARS

from Elton John and Tim Rice's AIDA

Music by ELTON JOHN
Lyrics by TIM RICE

To Coda

fail _____ to un-der-stand how a per-fect love ___ can be con-found - ed
wish _____ I nev - er learned what it is to be ___ in love and have that

out of hand. _____ *Both:* Is it writ - ten in the stars? ____ Are we

pay - ing for some crime? _ Is that all that we are good for, ___ just a

stretch of mor-tal time? _____ Is this God's ex - per - i - ment ____ in

YOU'LL BE IN MY HEART
(Pop Version)
from Walt Disney Pictures' TARZAN™

Words and Music by
PHIL COLLINS

Come stop your cry-ing; it will be all right.

Just take my hand, hold it tight. I will pro-tect you from

all a-round you. I will be here; don't you cry.

YOU ARE THE MUSIC IN ME

from the Disney Channel Original Movie HIGH SCHOOL MUSICAL 2

Words and Music by
JAMIE HOUSTON

Moderately fast Rock

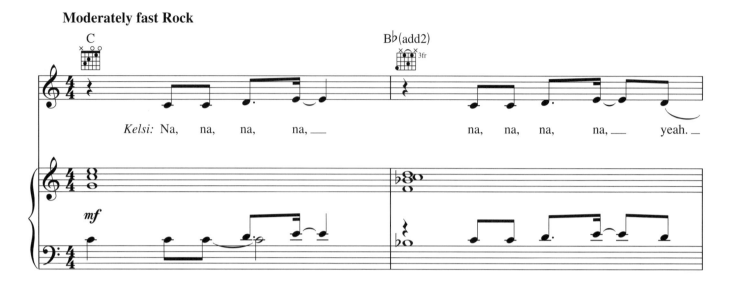

Kelsi: Na, na, na, na, na, na, na, na, yeah.

You are the mu-sic in me.

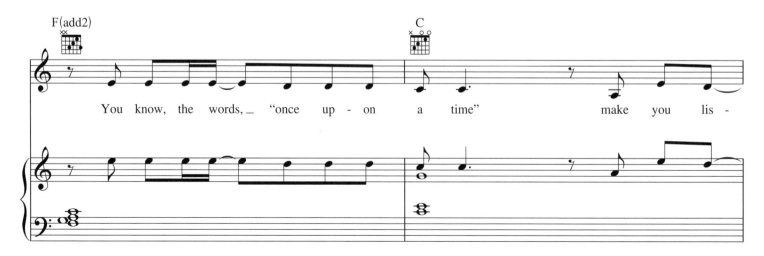

You know, the words, "once up-on a time" make you lis-